D1522233

THE

REDTAPE

LETTERS

**Confidential Letters from Redtape,
Leader of the Bureaucratic Party of
Canada, to Party Members**

Compiled by Preston Manning

PREFACE

Many of you may be familiar with *The Screwtape Letters* by C. S Lewis, the very wise and highly respected British philosopher and theologian. Screwtape is a senior devil writing to his nephew, a junior devil, and instructing him on strategic and practical ways to advance the cause of evil in the world. The book is funny, insightful and instructive – all at the same time.

Screwtape, for better or for worse, has inspired me to compile *The Redtape Letters.* These are confidential letters between *Redtape,* Leader of the Bureaucratic Party of Canada and the 325,000+ members of his party, instructing them on strategic and practical ways to ensure that the Bureaucratic Party of

Canada is and remains the largest and most powerful political party in the country.

Since Redtape apparently sent ten of these letters directly to over 325,000 federal bureaucrats – with no evident attempt or instruction to keep them secret – it is not surprising that copies ended up in the public domain and thereby became accessible to anyone including myself.

But it should be noted that Letter 3 – dealing with the training of Ministers and Prime Ministers – and Letter 9 dealing with the depersonalization of relations with persons served by the health, education, and social services departments of governments – were clearly marked as "strictly confidential". These were sent only to very senior bureaucrats and were obviously not intended for public disclosure.

The fact that copies of these letters were nevertheless leaked to me by certain recipients is an encouraging sign that not all bureaucrats – even those in senior positions and most trusted by Redtape – accepted his advice or supported his leadership.

This became particularly evident by the unexpected event that led to the composition and distribution of Letter 12 – the surprising content of which I shall leave to the reader to discover.

Preston Manning
Calgary, Alberta
May 2022

CONTENTS

Letter Number 12

June 15, 2023: Surprise, Surprise, Surprise!

Letter Number 1: June 1, 2022
The Party and Our Agenda

Dear Fellow Bureaucrats:

Greetings from the Nation's capital.

In this letter I want to give you a brief overview of our current position as a Party, which is stronger and more encouraging than ever before, and the key items on our agenda which will be the subject of future letters.

As you well know, the Bureaucratic Party of Canada, of which I am privileged to be the Leader, is now by far the largest, best organized, and most influential political party in the country.

The second largest is the Media Party of Canada but its influence is impaired by the internal division between the traditional mass media and the newer and ever-expanding social media. In addition, the Media Party only influences government decisions and action slowly and indirectly through the imperfect shaping of public opinion, whereas we shape and influence governmental decisions and actions daily and directly. And of course, both our Bureaucratic Party and the Media Party are now much larger, more organized, better funded, and more influential than any of those obsolete, dysfunctional, traditional political parties which still squabble over who can sit where in what numbers in that archaic chamber called the House of Commons.

You will note that, in communicating with you, I describe ourselves as a "political" party which is an accurate description. We will nevertheless continue to vigorously perpetuate the myth that the federal bureaucracy is "non-political". This notion, however, is only meant for external consumption by the politicians and the public.

The truth – just among ourselves – is that we are very political. We have our own political principles such as Principle One – that the answer to every public issue and challenge is some action and expenditure by governments. And Principle Two – that government expenditures, to be spent through us and by us, must always increase regardless of whether or not there are sufficient revenues to cover them. Not to mention Principles Three through Ten pertaining to the increasing of taxation, regulation, public monopolization, and the depersonalization of public services while avoiding any responsibility for outcomes and sustaining our organization.

We have our own political views and positions on every issue which we must assiduously advance at every opportunity, while always murmuring "Yes Minister", "Whatever you say, Minister", and "Your will be done, Prime Minister."

And we have our political allies. These include hundreds of thousands of provincial and municipal bureaucrats, members of the public service unions, and of course the leaders and members of those political parties who subscribe to Principles One and Two. It is these political allies – such as federal Liberals and New Democrats –

whom we very much wish to achieve and remain in elected office because they dare not challenge us and are the easiest to manage.

But enough of these generalities, the main purpose of this letter is to remind you again of the numbers which prove our size and influence, and which are such a source of encouragement as we face the challenges ahead. These are:

Total Number of Federal Bureaucrats: **325,000+**

Total Number of Elected Members of Parliament: **338**

Total Number of Federal Cabinet Ministers: **39**

As you can see, the only hold that the electors and parliament of Canada have on our organization of 325,000+ members is through 39 Cabinet Ministers, half of them incompetent, and most of whom couldn't initially find the washrooms nearest their offices without our assistance.

While we must continue to assiduously foster the illusion that it is the elected officials who are in control, and that we are their obedient "servants", the truth is the very opposite and as your Leader I am wholly committed to defending and advancing that truth.

With respect to my agenda as Leader, in future letters I will provide useful insights on such subjects as:

- The development and use of our own special language, Bureaucratese.

- The training of politicians, including Ministers and Prime Ministers, so that they are in effect our servants rather than our masters, while maintaining the illusion of the opposite.

- How to prevent responsibility for negative outcomes of government decisions, policies, and actions from falling on members of our Party.

- How to sustain the existence of bureaucratic departments and agencies when the original reasons for their formation and organization have long ceased to exist.

- How to sustain the financial support of our Party through government overspending, deficit financing, and money printing, and to resist counter-productive policies such as cost cutting and budget balancing.

- How to expand the regulatory functions of government, to concentrate that function in our hands, and to increase our influence and control over the economy and society through vastly increasing the number and scope of regulations.

- How to sustain and even expand the monopoly or quasi-monopoly positions which we hold in many areas of government activity such as health care, and to resist any move towards "mixed systems" or privatization.

- How to further depersonalize our relationship with Canadians by classifying and categorizing them as cases, file numbers, tax cows (to be milked), and "statistics" as distinct from human beings – particularly in such areas as healthcare, education, and social services.

- How to deal with that minority of old-fashioned public servants amongst us who still cling to outmoded views of public "service" and civil service "professionalism", views incompatible with our Party's objectives and practices.

In the meantime, best wishes to all. And keep on "serving."

Yours sincerely,

Redtape
Leader, Bureaucratic Party of Canada

Letter Number 2: July 2, 2022
Our Language, Bureaucratese

Dear Fellow Bureaucrats:

Today I want to briefly discuss the all-important subject of language and its use by the members of the Bureaucratic Party of Canada.

Canada is of course officially bilingual – English and French – but from our standpoint, the most important language, which can be translated into either French or English, is Bureaucratese. Those of us who can communicate in English, French, and Bureaucratese are actually Tri- Lingual and should therefore qualify for a Linguistic Bonus which we are lobbying our fellow bureaucrat, the Commissioner of Official Languages, to provide.

Bureaucratese is distinguished by the fact that it takes more words to express something in Bureaucratese than in any other language known to humankind. Its use produces memos, letters, emails, and documents of exceedingly great length and complexity – the composition, distribution, storage, and interpretation of which creates many jobs and incomes for our members.

Members of the Bureaucratic Party of Canada may use plain English or French in communicating with each other. But in communicating with our political masters or the public, I strongly advise you to communicate only in Bureaucratese.

A second characteristic of Bureaucratese is that it is very difficult for the politician, the media, and the general public to understand. It is obviously in the interests of our Party to make our communications even less understandable and more incomprehensible as this will generate even more jobs and incomes for bureaucrats to interpret and explain.

There are two main ways to make Bureaucratese even harder to understand. The first of these is to make extensive use of abbreviations for agencies, programs, and forms – all confusing and befuddling to the public and requiring our help to interpret and explain. The Canada Revenue Agency, for example, - with such forms as RC343, RC243-SCH-A, T2SCH13, RC4614, RC7214, GST20, RC7220, T2SCH502, RC193, T106, T50135CH444 (this one's a beauty), 5013-SC, T2SCH58, T2SCH97, RC322, T1163, T2125, AGR-1SUM, and E432 - has done an excellent job in this area and I urge others of you to emulate their example.

Once the number of abbreviations used by each department of the federal bureaucracy exceeds some target number – say 15,000 – it is my intention to propose the creation of a Department of Abbreviation, Interpretation, and Explanation Services (DAIES). This will require the employment of many more public "servants" – I use the term loosely – who will then of course become members of the Bureaucratic Party of Canada (BPC).

But there is a second and even more effective way to make our use of Bureaucratese harder to understand – so that our interpretive and explanatory help is even more obviously required – and that is to frequently use words that no one has ever heard of and to build upon that foundation of ignorance. No better example of the use of this tool can be found than one utilized by the British bureaucrats who drafted the BNA Act of 1867.

In section 92, ss.7 of that statute, defining the powers and responsibilities of Canada's provincial governments, it states among other things that they are to establish, maintain, and manage "eleemosynary institutions" in and for the Province. Do any of you have even the faintest idea what an eleemosynary institution is? Is the word "eleemosynary" in the vocabulary of any modern politician, let alone the vocabulary of the media or the public? Do you think the first Premiers of the newly created provinces, or even the current Premiers, really knew or know what it means to be responsible for an eleemosynary institution? Of course not, and responding to that ignorance provides us with a great opportunity to expand the bureaucracy. Let me explain.

Politicians hate to admit that they don't know something people think they ought to know, so if I had been around to influence the first Premiers regarding their responsibilities for eleemosynary institutions, and wanting to nudge them in a bureaucracy-building direction, this is the approach I would have taken:

"Good morning, Premier. Redtape at your service, sir."

"Good morning Redtape. Good to see you, but what's this about the need for us to establish a new department?"

"Yes. It's required by the constitution, sir. As you know, it says your provincial government is responsible for establishing eleemosynary institutions and I was wondering when we were going to get around to doing so?

"Oh Yes, Redtape. Eleemosynary institutions. I've always believed our province should have them – I mean, what's a province without eleemosynary services? And I was planning on appointing Smith to be the Minister of Eleemosynary Institutions – what do you think?"

"Yes, Premier. Smith would be excellent. I believe her uncle even taught a course at McGill on The History of Eleemosynary Institutions. And what will Smith need to assist her in discharging her duties?"

"Well, I suppose the usual. You'll need to find her a Deputy, an Assistant Deputy, three Directors, some Assistant Directors, and dozens of front line eleemosynaries to deliver the program – all with eleemosynary experience of course. You know – the usual, and it's time to get at it."

"Yes, of course Premier. Your will be done, sir. A full-blown Department of Eleemosynary Institutions. Just what this province and country needs, sir."

You see my fellow bureaucrats, while this letter only touches the surface I hope it gives you a glimpse of how the proper use of brain-numbing Bureaucratese, liberally sprinkled with abbreviations and words that no one knows the meaning of, can be used to greatly expand our numbers and influence.

Yours sincerely,

Redtape
Leader, Bureaucratic Party of Canada

Letter Number 3: August 1, 2022
The Training of Ministers and Prime Ministers

Dear Senior Bureaucrats:

You will note at the outset that this particular letter is not directed to our rank and file members but only to those of you in senior positions – those who work directly with Ministers and the Prime Minister. The reasons for this focus will become obvious as you read on, and this communication must be treated as confidential and destroyed after you have absorbed its contents.

As you well know, following an election – particularly if it results in a change of government – we will be presented with a fresh crop of Ministers, and perhaps even a new Prime Minister, with very little knowledge or experience of the portfolios and public duties which they will now be responsible for discharging.

It is then our unenviable responsibility, as the permanent public service, to show these political transients the washrooms closest to their new offices and everything else they need to know to stay out of administrative or political trouble and appear to be delivering Peace, Order, and Good Government.

To assist you in the discharge of this responsibility, the Bureaucratic Party of Canada has assembled a Manual for the Training of Ministers and Prime Ministers (MTMPM) which is available in both official languages from my office upon request. The existence and content of this manual is to be treated as confidential, but I assure you it will be very useful to you in performing this training function.

Some of you may ask: "But what if my Minister is one of these cocksure politicos who thinks he/she already knows everything about running a government department and eschews my help?" This is a perennial problem and is addressed in Chapter 2 of the Manual under the heading of "Getting Your Minister's Attention".

The technique is very simple: let your Minister get into "trouble" – especially political trouble. Even help your Minister to get into trouble by suggesting he/she do something in an area fraught with problems of which he/she is unaware, or providing your Minister with an intemperate or error-infected speech which once delivered will generate negative blowback from the media and the public.

Once your Minister finds himself/herself in "trouble", who can he/she turn to for "help" but you - his/her faithful deputy and obedient servant, always willing and able to be of assistance? Once your Minister is thoroughly obligated to you in this way, he/she will be much more open to "training".

But – and this is a "Big But" that I never anticipated needing to address. In the last few years the background and nature of the politicos we have to deal with at the senior level, and whom we need to prepare for office, has completely changed.

It really began with the election of a certain Prime Minister in 2015 and the later appointment of a certain Finance Minister in 2020. (Names are not really important as these people come and go.) The Prime Minister in question had briefly been a teacher and was also an amateur actor with no prior training or experience in the functions of a Prime Minister or even those of a Cabinet Minister. When he then became Prime Minister, it was of course too late for him to acquire such training and experience. So what we had was an amateur actor *playing the role of Prime Minister*, as in a movie or TV series, and the training required was not pertaining to being an actual Prime Minister but *how to play the role of Prime Minister* as impressively and believably as possible.

The same situation presented itself in 2020 when a former journalist – no doubt sincere and well meaning – was appointed Finance

Minister. As you will know, it is possible to get an advanced degree in Journalism from graduate schools in this country like Ryerson or Carleton without having taken even one course in economics or public finance. You also know from experience how easy it is to mislead members of the Ottawa press gallery on the state of government finances because of the deficiencies in their knowledge and experience in this area.

In any event, in the case of this Finance Minister, the preparation and training that we were in a position to provide did not pertain, as in the old days, to running the Finance Department. No, what we now needed to provide was preparation and training that would equip the Minister *to play the role of Finance Minister* as effectively and impressively as possible –

while, of course, we of the bureaucracy ran the department.

To do this we had to completely revamp, in both official languages, the MTMPM (Manual for the Training of Ministers and Prime Ministers) and we had to hire as trainers – not experts in government and public finance, but those from the entertainment industry skilled in preparing and training actors to play their roles as believably and credibly as possible.

Lest you have some skepticism about the effectiveness of this kind of training, I would simply invite you to carefully watch some of the top medical series on television – House, The Good Doctor, Grey's Anatomy – you know the ilk. The doctors, nurses, and other health care professionals who appear on these shows are not what they appear to be – they are actors *playing the roles* of doctors, nurses, and healthcare professionals. But note how well they do it. They look, talk, and act like the real thing. They even appear to be quite capable of performing complicated and advanced medical procedures and operations so realistically you would swear they are "the real thing". But of course they are not. They are actors professionally prepared and trained to role play and it is our task to provide the same kind and level of training to the politicos in our care so that they can play the roles of Prime Minister and Cabinet Ministers with the same degree of professionalism and believability.

I have gone on for too long, but one more thing before I close. It is absolutely essential, as I stressed at the beginning of this communication, that this memo and the new focus of our training be kept strictly confidential. None of us in our right mind would ever trust those actors in the medical shows to actually operate on us if we had a personal medical condition requiring treatment. Similarly, voters in their right minds would never trust the politicians we have trained to actually manage a government or a department if they knew those politicians were essentially just political actors playing a role. Please therefore destroy this communication as soon as you have absorbed its contents.

Yours sincerely,

Redtape
Leader, Bureaucratic Party of Canada

Letter Number 4: September 3, 2022 Avoiding Responsibility and Accountability

One of the most important political and governmental myths in Canada which it is very much in our interests to maintain, is that the country enjoys "responsible government". The concept – vigorously fought to be the early Reformers of Upper and Lower Canada such as Baldwin and LaFontaine, and Joseph Howe in Nova Scotia – is that governments are responsible and accountable to those who elect them and that the Executive is responsible and accountable to the elected legislature.

In practice, however, the majority of elected officials today accept responsibility and accountability for their policies and actions only "when things go well". But when "things go wrong", which more than often is the case, they scrupulously seek to avoid responsibility and accountability. Of course, the easiest way for them to do so is to blame us, the members of the bureaucracy.

It is this characteristic of the political world that has caused the Bureaucratic Party of Canada, in the interests of all our members, to develop our own Policy on Responsibility and Accountability for the conduct and outcomes of governmental policies and actions with which we are involved.

In a nutshell, this Policy is simply this: To accept no responsibility whatsoever for governmental mismanagement or negative outcomes arising from the actions or policies of governments of which we are a part, and to organize and conduct ourselves in such a way that none of our members, individually or collectively, can ever be held accountable in any way, shape, or form for any such mismanagement or negative outcomes.

How do we accomplish this? Let me explain. First of all, we promote the creation of *multiple vertical layers* of government organization between the public "out there" and the political minister at the top of the government – with layers and layers of service providers, administrators, supervisors, program heads, directors, advisors, assistant deputy ministers, deputy ministers, etc. in between. Most of these are nameless and faceless public servants and hard for the public or media to identify, so if anything goes wrong in serving the public "out there", the easiest and most visible person to blame is the Minister up top, not us in-between bureaucrats.

And then we divide responsibility for whatever governments do *horizontally* into multiple departments, agencies, crown corporations, etc. In fact, the more there are of these departments, agencies and crown corporations the better because it divides governmental responsibility for anything ever more finely. And thus, in the end, responsibility for the consequences of government actions is divided so finely, both vertically and horizontally, that "when things go wrong", it becomes impossible to determine who is responsible and should be held accountable – least of all those of us in the bureaucracy.

This then is our Policy on Responsibility and Accountability and how we go about implementing it. Clever, don't you think? Sort of "liability insurance" for bureaucrats. Please support and expand its application every chance you get.

Yours "protectively",

Redtape

Leader, Bureaucratic Party of Canada

Letter Number 5: October 3, 2022
Sustaining Bureaucracy

Dear Fellow Bureaucrats:

As I have told you before, the strength of the Bureaucratic Party of Canada is in our numbers – in our size, currently, 325,000 and counting. Our numbers must never be allowed to decrease – only increase.

So what is to be done if the need for a particular government program, agency, or department populated and managed by bureaucrats like ourselves, no longer exists - what then? If such programs, agencies or departments are wound up, the Bureaucratic Party of Canada is weakened – something we cannot allow to happen. So what is to be done?

Two strategies commend themselves: (1) Resist and delay any attempted reduction in size or elimination of any government program, agency, or department as long as possible, and, (2) Find new purposes for any unneeded programs, agencies, or departments rather than allowing them to be wound up.

For example, you will be amazed as to how successful our bureaucratic forefathers have been in the past in practicing the resist and delay strategy. The archives of the Bureaucratic Party contain a file describing how they were able to keep the Pony Express division of Canada Post – including its blacksmith shops and stables – in operation until 1932 despite all the more modern methods of moving letters and parcels which had come on the scene.

And with respect to the second strategy – repurposing a bureaucracy for future growth rather than allowing it to be wound down – we have an excellent example on the international scene right now. The United Nations was conceived first and foremost as a peacekeeping organization after the Second World War. A large and growing bureaucracy was built up to support its operations and it had some initial successes, for example, in dealing with the Suez crisis of 1956.

But over time, despite the increasing size and complexity of the UN bureaucracy and budget, it proved less and less successful in fulfilling its original purpose – unable to prevent or stop the Vietnam war, civil wars in Nigeria (Biafra) and Rwanda, major conflicts in the Balkans or Middle East, or the current military attacks on the Ukraine by Russia, a member of its own Security Council.

Rumblings were heard in the international community that the UN might well go the way of the League of Nations and disappear into the ash bin of history. But that would have been a catastrophe, not necessarily for the world, but certainly for the UN bureaucracy whose preservation and expansion had become its number one priority. A new raison d'etre had to be found, but what could it be? How about combating Climate Change? The UN would focus, not on reducing wars but on reducing carbon dioxide emissions, saving the UN bureaucracy on the pretext of saving the planet.

Members of the Bureaucratic Party of Canada, take heed! If the bureaucracies of the federal, provincial, or municipal governments, of which you are a part, are faced by anything that might halt their growth or even cause them to be reduced in size – fight tooth and nail to prevent any structural reform with that object in mind. And if the purpose for which your bureaucracy was originally formed is no longer sufficient to sustain its growth and our membership therein, find a new purpose – any purpose, but preferably one with both virtue signaling possibilities and growth potential – so that our Party is guaranteed sustainability and future growth.

Yours sincerely,
Redtape
Leader, Bureaucratic Party of Canada

Letter Number 6: November 2, 2022
Spend, Tax, Borrow!

Dear Fellow Bureaucrats:

As the Leader of The Bureaucratic Party of Canada – our country's largest and most influential political party – let me again thank you for your support.

This month, I want to remind you of one of our Party's most important policy positions, namely our Fiscal Policy. In a nutshell, it is to promote and support increased government spending whenever possible, and increased taxation and government borrowing to sustain that increased spending.

The reasons for strongly advancing this policy are obvious since increasing government spending means a larger public sector with more public servants like ourselves with higher incomes. This policy also increases the human and financial resources at our disposal as managers of the public sector, thus increasing our influence in the economy and society.

I must warn you, however, that there are those in the elected legislatures who would frustrate the implementation of our Fiscal Policy by the odious advocacy of cost cutting and budget balancing, and who steadfastly resist the increases in taxes and borrowings necessary to sustain that increased spending.

There is a strategy, however, for dealing effectively with these cost cutters and budget balancers and it is best illustrated by the following incident: A former Prime

Minister, best known for profligate spending, was stricken late in his term by the budget-balancing virus and ordered his Finance Minister to balance the budget by cutting costs. So the Finance Minister summoned his Deputy, one of our colleagues, and ordered him to produce a list of 20 major government expenditures which could be cut immediately to reduce costs. The Deputy returned several hours later with the list, but when the Minister reviewed it he expressed surprise, saying: "This is a great list, but the number one item on it is a large park facility in my riding." To which our colleague sagely replied, "Minister, any and every cut is always in somebody's riding."

So, the strategy employed here is that when a government asks for budget balancing through cost cutting, we in the bureaucracy must respond if at all possible by cutting the programs and services which will be most visible, painful, and politically damaging to the government, especially the cost cutting advocates among its ministers and supporters. Cuts to programs servicing widows, orphans, the sick, disabled persons, and visible minorities are especially effective in this regard.

But pursuing the Fiscal Policy of the Bureaucratic Party encounters yet another challenge in that these political fanatics who urge cost cutting and budget balancing are usually in the forefront of also urging tax reductions.

Recently one of these political Neanderthals even introduced a private member's bill in the House of Commons calling for the government to change the name of the esteemed Canadian Revenue Agency (CRA) to the Ottawa Looting and Pillaging Company. Our Liberal and NDP allies in the House will of course ensure the defeat of this bill, but the fact that it was even proposed is an indication of an anti-taxation sentiment which must be constantly guarded against and opposed.

The CRA is of course the home and workplace of tens of thousands of dedicated members of the Bureaucratic Party of Canada. Due to our efforts to promote and expand its work, the CRA now has a greater numbers of employees than the Canadian Armed Forces and has even more sophisticated electronic equipment and management systems to enable it to detect and pursue tax evaders whom we regard as more dangerous to the wellbeing of the federation and ourselves than any external enemy.

As Party members will know, I am scheduled to give a major address at our Party's annual convention next spring. One of our most brilliant colleagues in the communications section of the Department of National Revenue has suggested that it should include a passionate restatement of our Party's commitment to increased taxation. He has even suggested some appropriate language (I'm not sure where he got this), a portion of which I share with you here on a confidential basis:

We shall not flag nor fail. We shall tax on the beaches and on the land. We shall tax on the hills and in the valleys. We shall tax in the fields and the forests. We shall tax in the streets, the stores, the offices, the factories, and the homes of the nation. We shall tax anything that moves and also that which does not move. We shall never reduce, we will never rebate, and we shall tax until 70% or more of the nation's income comes into our hands and passes through them to achieve the great and benevolent objectives that we in the Bureaucratic Party are best qualified to determine and pursue. . .

I share these words with you now, as an inspiration and encouragement for each and every one of you to persevere in pursuit of our Party's Fiscal Policy – ever increasing public spending and ever increasing taxation and borrowing to support it.

With best regards,

Redtape
Leader, Bureaucratic Party of Canada

Letter Number 7: December 6, 2022
Regulate, Regulate, Regulate

Dear Fellow Bureaucrats:

Greetings again from the Nation's capital, stronghold of the federal bureaucracy.

Today, I am visiting federal offices at Tunney's Pasture – 121 acres of land in Ottawa, owned by Canada Lands, exclusively devoted to federal government buildings, and home to over 13,000 of our members.

In visiting here, I am reminded that from time to time federal politicians are seized with the "decentralization fever" – an urge to decentralize the programs and offices of the federal government rather than concentrate as many of them as possible here in Ottawa. This noxious fever sometimes emanates from Quebecers who want decentralization for cultural and social reasons or from Westerners who want decentralization for economic reasons. But it is worrisome nevertheless from the standpoint of the Bureaucratic Party of Canada because we are much stronger when our bureaucratic presence is concentrated by centralization rather than diluted through decentralization.

I'm reminded in visiting here that several decades ago a troublesome consultant from the west had the audacity to author a paper entitled *May The Cows Graze Again in Tunney's Pasture*. Fortunately, we were successful in countering it, his decentralization initiative failed, and the BPA (Bureaucrats Per Acre) ratio for the

pasture today is a healthy 107
(13,000/121=107) and rising.

But I digress. What I want to emphasize and share with you today is that one of the key objectives of our Party and a major plank in our Party Platform is **to increase regulation** – federal, provincial, municipal, industrial, financial, social, and every other kind of regulation.

This is of great importance because the power and influence of bureaucracy and our Party is directly proportional to the number and nature of government regulations.

What this means – especially for those of you in positions to influence the drafting of bills establishing or governing departments, agencies, and programs – is that *you must ensure that there is always a section in every such statute providing for the making and enforcing of Regulations.*

Such clauses must be worded in such a way as to reinforce the legal fiction that it is only the Minister or the Lieutenant Governor or Governor General in Council (the Cabinet) who are empowered to make and enforce regulations. We, the bureaucrats, are not and should not even be mentioned.

Of course, the truth is that the Minister and/or the Cabinet have neither the interest nor the time to even read let alone administer the hundreds and hundreds of regulations spawned by these sections. It is we, the bureaucrats who suggest them, draft them, read them, amend them, enforce them and replace them from time to time with newer and better regulations and who in reality wield the regulatory authority.

Therein lies our great power to shape and direct the affairs of state, the economy, and the society and we must never relinquish it. The statutory authority to make regulations is the Magna Carta of Bureaucracy.

To cite but one example from the Ontario jurisdiction, The People's Health Care Act, 2019, consists of 12 Parts and 51 sections. But the part of greatest meaning and use to the Ontario chapter of the Bureaucratic Party of Canada is Part VII labeled *regulations* and containing section 41 (1) which declares that: "The Lieutenant Governor in Council may make regulations."

The section then goes on in 15 subsections to specify in delicious detail all the various activities to be regulated under the Act. The Lieutenant Governor in Council may make regulations specifying this, exempting that, prescribing provisions to do this or that – to make regulations governing funding, governing many other things, allowing whatever, disallowing whatever, and defining words and expressions to be used. It ends wonderfully by granting an omnibus power to make regulations "respecting any other matter that the Lieutenant Governor in Council considers necessary or desirable for carrying out the purposes and provisions of this Act."

One further admonition: never let any regulation die if you can possibly help it, as the number of bureaucrats employed to regulate is directly related to the number of regulations. One area where we have been spectacularly successful in preserving the enforcement of a regulation that has long outlived its usefulness is with respect to the seat belt regulation originally imposed on Trans Canada Airlines (now Air Canada). This regulation, formulated in the early days of air travel, requires that prior to every flight, passengers should not only be required to buckle up a seat belt, *but shown how to do so.*

According to the research department of the Bureaucratic Party of Canada, some 62,347,304 demonstrations of how to do up a seat belt have been given to air-traveling Canadians in compliance with this single regulation.

Recent polling of a large representative sample of Canadians on this issue showed that 99.64% of respondents answered "Yes" to the question, "Do you know how to do up a seat belt?" And 99.03% also answered "Yes" to the question "If you were sitting next to someone in an airplane and they didn't know how to do up their seat belt, would you show them how?" There was a danger, however, that such scientific information might lead to abandonment of the regulation still requiring Canadians to be shown how to do up their seat belts every time they get on an airplane. But fortunately, from the standpoint of the Bureaucratic Party of Canada, this dimension of the science of seat belt use has been ignored and the attendants on passenger airplanes are still required by regulation to show Canadians what? - How to do up their seat belts.

What more can I say, fellow bureaucrats. Regulations are a bureaucrat's best friend, so demand them, make them, multiply them, enforce them, defend them, and

preserve them even when they are obsolete.
Regulate, regulate, regulate!

Yours sincerely,

Redtape

Leader, Bureaucratic Party of Canada

Letter Number 8: January 2, 2023 Champion Public Enterprise and Public Monopolies

Dear Fellow Bureaucrats:

Greetings again from the National Capital Region where the BPA ratio (Bureaucrats Per Acre) is the highest in the country.

I very much appreciate receiving feedback from you, in particular your inquiries and suggestions Re: the positions of the Bureaucratic Party of Canada on important themes. And one of those which I want to address in this letter is the need for our Party to constantly champion public enterprises and public monopolies.

As you will know from studying our Party's Policy Manual, we are very much in favor of such enterprises, especially public monopolies and quasi-monopolies, because it is members of our Party who direct and populate them to our great benefit from the standpoint of employment, income, and influence.

One of the most important of these is the quasi-monopoly given to the federal and provincial governments in the area of Public Health, where statutes such as the Canada Health Act and provincial Health Acts severely limit participation by non-government entities (charitable organizations, not-for-profit companies, and for-profit enterprises) in the sector.

Governments in Canada also enjoy quasi-monopoly status in the areas of Public Education and Social Services, but regrettably I must warn you that our privileged status in all three of these areas is threatened.

For some strange reason that I fail to understand, there appears to be a growing public appetite for "freedom of choice" in all of these areas. In the health care sector this has been prompted by the allegation – which we must refute whether it is true or not – that countries with "mixed" (public and private) health care systems responded more quickly and effectively to the recent COVID crisis than did our Canadian system. But there is also increased agitation for "mixed" systems in the educational and social services spheres as well.

Let me assure you, as the leader of the Bureaucratic Party whose members currently dominate these sectors and operate them to our own benefit, that I hate competition as strongly as any private monopolist and will do everything in my power to resist this retrograde movement toward more competition. In this struggle, I earnestly request your wholehearted support.

Looking ahead, there is another extremely important sphere, where the battle between public sector dominance and control, and private sector competition, has not yet been won by those of us who favor public enterprises and public monopolies operated by public bureaucracies. And that is the sphere of climate change and environmental protection.

Those of us in the Bureaucratic Party believe that it is the public sector which should be in charge, to the maximum extent possible, of measures to conserve the environment and prevent climate change. But there are those in the business and political community who believe that market mechanisms – entrepreneurship, private capital, and market based pricing regimes – could and should also be harnessed to environmental protection.

As you know, we have been largely successful in assuming control over the development and non-development of the natural resource sectors – agriculture, energy, mining, forestry, and fisheries – by throttling them in red tape. But "the environment" is the greatest natural resource sector of all and our aim must be to gain full control of it by wrapping it in green tape – all in the name of fighting climate change.

One of the most effective ways of doing this is to require Environmental Impact Assessments of every single human activity, except of course the activities of public bureaucracies and the governments of which we are a part, and to require those assessments to be submitted to bureaucratically organized and controlled Regulatory Tribunals capable of taking months to evaluate and act upon them. But we must also resist this pernicious suggestion, surfacing in some jurisdictions, that Economic Impact Assessments should be done on every environmental protection regulation we advance, as this might well constrain our efforts to assume total control over the "environmental sector".

One final thought which relates to our objective of expanding the public sector in every way possible. Most of you share my contempt for those traditional political parties whom we have largely replaced, but some of you have asked whether it might still be to our advantage as bureaucrats to support at least one of them – whichever one is most easily harnessed to our objectives.

My response is to say that if we are to encourage or support any of those parties – strictly to advance our own interests – it would be that so-called "New Democratic Party". This particular party often claims to be a "worker's party" and promises, like all parties, that if elected to government it will "create jobs". But when NDP governments on occasion have been elected provincially, their election chases away private capital so the job-creating capacity of the private sector is reduced rather than increased. For example, when Ontario briefly suffered the one term election of an NDP government under a Mr. Rae, he was actually nominated for "Businessman of the Year" in Buffalo New York because of the large volume of job-creating private capital from Ontario that he drove into Buffalo.

So, what is such an NDP government to do to fulfill its "we will create jobs" promise? There are only two things it can do – expand the civil service by hiring more bureaucrats like us and undertake massive public works projects again requiring more bureaucrats like us to manage.

I know that many of you resist voting in elections because of your contempt for all the options offered. But when such elections come along, I urge you to hold your noses and support the NDP – their leaders and candidates are most easily harnessed to the expansion of the public sector and our goal of creating the authoritarian Bureaucratic state.

Yours sincerely,

Redtape
Leader, Bureaucratic Party of Canada

Letter Number 9: February 5, 2023 Depersonalize, Depersonalize, Depersonalize!

Dear Fellow Bureaucrats:

This letter is being sent only to those of you who work in the health, education, and social service departments and agencies of government – the "people" departments and agencies. Its content must be treated as highly confidential because, if it were to get out to the media or the general public, that would seriously undermine confidence in the "welfare state" – a state where the welfare of the government bureaucracy is the highest priority and which we have labored so long and hard to create and sustain.

As all of us well know, the bureaucracies of which we are a part and on which we depend for our jobs, incomes, and status in society are very good at collecting and transmitting to political decision makers information which can be objectively measured and quantified – population figures, GDP numbers, unemployment numbers, taxes owed/taxes paid numbers, and the numbers and other quantifiable characteristics of persons in schools, in hospitals, on healthcare waiting lines, on welfare, and among the population generally.

But we must acknowledge – and I hate to admit this – that bureaucracies are not so good at collecting and accurately transmitting other types of information – that pertaining to emotions, values, hopes, fears, personal relationships, community relationships and all the experiences that shape these – precisely the kind of information that is needed to deal "humanely" as distinct from "mechanistically" with human beings, especially those with particular problems and needs. This is why we in the bureaucracy reduce, wherever and whenever possible, the human subjects we must deal with – especially in the fields of education, healthcare, and social services – to "files and cases" to which impersonal numbers can be assigned and which makes them "manageable" by our structures and processes.

If politicians and public policy advocates ever get it into their heads to try to "personalize" government services and to make the relationship between governments and the population more "humane", this would be a huge blow to the size and influence of the Bureaucratic Party of Canada. Such efforts must therefore be strenuously resisted. In fact we in the bureaucracy must redouble our efforts to move things in the opposite direction – to further depersonalize relations between government and those we "serve" until even the most naïve idealists see that "personalizing" government is a hopeless quest.

To assist us in this effort, our research department has developed the Bureaucratic App (BAP for short) and I urge every one of you to download it at once. Once you have it, whenever you encounter a recipient of your government service, whatever that may be, all you do is type in their name and BAP will give you the number used to identify them in our bureaucratic system –

their BUNU (short for Bureaucratic Number) as we call it. After that, whenever you communicate with them – by letter, email, but even by phone or in person – use their BUNU as often as possible, and gradually, if we persist, they will begin to think of themselves, not by their personal name, but by the number by which the great, benevolent, government bureaucracy knows and serves them.

Impossible, you say, to carry our Depersonalization Policy to this length? Rubbish! We just need to persist. If people can remember their nine digit cell phone number they can memorize their nine or ten digit BUNU. I have a nephew whose parents named him Wilbur Marvin Johnson but whose BUNU is 756 490 221. For the last six months I've been calling him by his bureaucratic nickname 756-4, and today he responds immediately when I call it out.

You smile, but this is serious. If our Depersonalization Policy is frustrated or reversed, then – mark my words the days of the Bureaucratic Party of Canada being in power are numbered.

Yours sincerely,

Redtape
Leader, Bureaucratic Party of Canada

**Letter Number 10: March 2, 2023
Defeating the Anti-Bureaucratic Party**

Dear Fellow Bureaucrats:

It pains me to write this letter to you because it deals with a most unpleasant matter – the regrettable fact that there is an odious minority among the members of the great Bureaucratic Party of Canada who do not share the objectives and views that I have been communicating to you and who appear to desire alternative leadership to that which I provide.

The members of this odious minority cling to outmoded views of what it means to be a "civil servant". They attach inordinate weight to the concept of "service" – apparently believing that we truly ought to "serve" the public and the officials they elect rather than aiming for their mastery which has been the principal objective of my leadership.

You can tell these reactionaries by their speech – they prefer to speak clear and plain English or French to the public and politicians rather than communicating in the Bureaucratese that I recommend. They refuse to cultivate the dependency-creating relationship with Ministers which is the aim of our Manual for the Training of Ministers and Prime Ministers (MTMAPM), and even accept responsibility rather than scrupulously avoiding it when "things go wrong". They do not enthusiastically support the aims of our spend, borrow, and tax Fiscal Policy nor the concepts of multiplying regulations, protecting and expanding public monopolies, and accelerating the depersonalization of our relations with Canadians especially in the social service domain.

In short, they contend that such political positions, which I have worked so long and hard to advance on your behalf, *ought not to be* the positions of "professional" civil servants. It is even rumored that they will contest my leadership at the next annual Convention of our Party by putting forward some woman named Notape as a candidate for my replacement.

As I said at the beginning of this letter, it pains me to even recognize the existence of this reactionary minority, let alone be forced to defend my leadership against them. But make no mistake, defend and advance my leadership and the principles and policies on which it is based is exactly what I intend to do.

My next communication with you will therefore be a clear enunciation of the progressive platform on which I stand and on which I will seek your support at our next Party convention slated for early June of this year. I shall even propose that those archaic democratic elements of our Party's Constitution, which encourage diversity of thought and weaken the status and power of the Leader, be purged from that Constitution, so that it becomes a true foundation for the authoritative Bureaucratic State we seek to create.

Yours truly,

Redtape
Leader, Bureaucratic Party of Canada

Letter Number 11: April 5, 2023
The Bureaucrat's Manifesto

Dear Fellow Bureaucrats:

In my last letter to you, dated March 2, 2023, I warned you of the existence of a reactionary minority among our membership who do not support the progressive policies of the Bureaucratic Party of Canada, and may even seek my replacement as Leader at our next Party convention.

I also promised you a clear enunciation of the principles and platform on which I will stand for re-election, so here they are:

Principles:

1.   That government of the bureaucracy, by the bureaucracy, and for the bureaucracy is the ideal form of government.

2.   That the answer to every public issue and challenge is some action and expenditure by bureaucratically controlled governments.

3.   That government expenditures, to be spent by and through the bureaucracy, must always increase regardless of whether or not there are sufficient revenues to cover them.

4.   That increasing the numbers and complexities of bureaucratic

regulations, and increasing the numbers and bureaucratic control of public enterprises and monopolies, are always in the public interest.

5.   That distant and impersonal relations, between the recipients of government services and those of the bureaucracies providing them, are infinitely preferable to humane and difficult-to-control personal relations.

6.   That change and an accelerated pace of change, except when initiated and controlled by the bureaucracy, is to be steadfastly resisted.

7.   That creating, sustaining, and expanding the reach of the authoritative Bureaucratic State is

the highest and most worthy goal to
be pursued politically and
administratively.

Platform

These are the measures I will seek to
implement if re-elected as the Leader of the
Bureaucratic Party of Canada for another
term:

1.   Increasing the size of the federal
       bureaucracy to more than 500,000
       members and increasing the BPA
       (Bureaucrats per Acre) in every
       provincial capital by 15%.

2.   Instituting mandatory language
       training in the proper use of
       Bureaucratese for new public service
       hires and increasing the numbers

and volume of federal government forms by 10% per department.

3. Putting the training of new Ministers completely into the hands of those skilled in training movie and television actors and replacing speech writers with script writers.

4. Adding two more horizontal layers of organization (3 more departments) and three more vertical dimensions (3 new organizational layers) to the federal bureaucracy.

5. Eliminating all sunset clauses from federal legislation so that no existing federal program or agency, however obsolete and useless, shall cease to exist during my next term.

6.   Providing under-the-table aid and support to any candidate for public office who will pledge to support increased public spending and taxation, to oppose any cost cutting or attempted budget balancing, and to support continued expansion of public enterprise, public monopolies, and the public sector.

7.   Strangling with regulation and increased taxation any private sector involvement in the health, education, and social services sectors so that public entities employing myriads of bureaucrats will enjoy a virtual monopoly in these sectors.

8.   Making it mandatory to, first and foremost, refer to anyone receiving

government services by their
government designated number
(their BUNU) rather than by name.

9. Purging from all committees,
sub-committees, and other
organizational units of the
Bureaucratic Party of Canada any
member who adheres to heretical
and anti-bureaucratic views such as
civil "service" and old-fashioned
"professionalism".

10.	Removing from our Party's Constitution those archaic democratic elements which encourage diversity of thought, weaken the status and power of the Leader, and impede the establishment of the authoritative Bureaucratic State.

It is on the basis of these principles and platform elements that I seek your wholehearted and enthusiastic support, that I may continue as the Leader and guide of the great Bureaucratic Party of Canada.

Yours sincerely,

Redtape
Leader, Bureaucratic Party of Canada

Letter Number 12: June 15, 2023
Surprise, Surprise, Surprise!

Dear Fellow Members of the Canadian Civil Service:

By now you will be fully aware of the surprising results of the recent election to determine the next Leader of the Bureaucratic Party of Canada: The fact that our former Leader, Redtape, was defeated in his bid for re-election, and that I, Notape, was duly elected to take his place.

I wish to take this opportunity to sincerely thank each and every one of you who supported me and my platform of Civil Service Reform. But I also want to take this opportunity to assure those of you who did not support me that there will be no reprisals or recriminations as, hopefully, we all move forward together.

On your behalf, I also want to wish Redtape well as he visits North Korea to receive the Kim Jong-un Award for the Advancement of Authoritarian Bureaucratism, and as he takes his new position, just announced, as a Public Service Advisor to the Government of Cuba.

As promised in my campaign, my first initiatives will be to de-register the Bureaucratic Party of Canada as a federal political party and to create in its place several Public Servants Associations offering different perspectives and services – any one of which you will be free to join.

My second initiative will be to institute a process of Civil Service Reform whereby we shall seek to establish a genuine "service ethic" within the federal civil service, to foster a genuine "service commitment" on the part of our members in our dealings with Canadians, and to humanize and personalize our relations with Canadians whom we are dedicated to serve.

My third initiative will be to institute a complete review of the policies promoted by my predecessor with an aim to examining and revising them in the light of these new commitments which you endorsed by electing me as your new Leader. This review is likely to result in:

- The reinstitution of plain English or French as the languages of the federal civil service and the abandonment of Bureaucratese.

- Replacement of the Manual for the Training of Ministers and Prime Ministers with a manual for the training of civil servants to provide genuine and useful service to such Ministers.

- A responsibility and accountability commitment whereby public servants accept rather than avoid taking responsibility for our recommendations and actions.

- The reinstitution of sunset clauses in legislation establishing programs and agencies, so that those no longer needed will cease to exist.

- A commitment on the part of public servants to efficiency and fiscal responsibility, including the balancing of budgets.

- An absolute reduction in the volume and intrusiveness of federal regulation.

- The elimination of public monopolies and a welcoming of constructive competition.

- The personalization of our relations with Canadians who are the recipients of our services and who pay our salaries and provide our benefits and pensions.

In closing, I want to acknowledge that under the leadership of the past, our reputation and status as public servants was tarnished and diminished, despite the claim that our power and prestige was increasing.

We came to be known by the common people as "bureaucrats" – cold, self-serving functionaries dedicated solely to the advancement of our own interests and more feared for the influence we wielded than respected for the services we provided.

My objective, with the mandate you have given me, is to change all that through Civil Service Reform. To do so, I need your help, ideas, suggestions, cooperation, and support – all of which I earnestly solicit through this, my first official communication with you.

Yours sincerely,

Notape
Leader, of the soon to be de-registered, Bureaucratic Party of Canada

Made in United States
North Haven, CT
20 November 2022

27011299R00055